FIND YOUR OWN STYLE

Frederica Lord

Introduced by Prudence Glynn, fashion editor of 'The Times'

Macdonald

Editorial manager
Chester Fisher
Series editor
Jim Miles
Editor
Linda Sonntag
Designer
Peter Benoist
Picture researcher
Anne Williams
Production
Penny Kitchenham

Published in association with Thames Television's pro-
gramme *After Noon*, produced by Catherine Freeman

First published 1978
Macdonald Educational Ltd
Holywell House
Worship Street
London EC2A 2EN

ISBN 356 06201 5

Made and printed by
Waterlows (Dunstable) Ltd

Contents

Introduction

Be honest. How often have you come out of a shop cross and disgruntled, muttering 'they don't have a very good choice in *there'*, when what you really mean is that the choice was far too wide? That you were in fact baffled by the selection? That you couldn't decide whether to opt for the frilly, the ethnic, the tailored, a one-piece, two-piece, three-piece? In short: you wanted guidance.

Guidance is something many women find lacking these days in fashion, because there are so many ways to look good, and so many ways, you can't help thinking, to look a downright mess. It was much easier when the magazine editors and the designers decided it all for you.

And this is why this book is a must, because it sets you on course to find your own style for yourself. You don't need to spend a fortune or so much as dip into the housekeeping budget. Once you have discovered your type and recognized your good points as well as your bad, you'll be able to make the most of what you've got. And that's what fashion is all about.

Prudence Glynn, fashion editor of 'The Times'

◀ *Author Frederica Lord chats with London designer*
Zandra Rhodes prior to her appearance on After Noon.

The style of our times

Fashion comes and goes—style is how you wear it. Throughout human history the clothing and appearance of most women (and men and children) has changed little and slowly. Today there are still remote parts of the world where clothing has not changed for hundreds of years, whereas our own fashions have changed increasingly rapidly since the turn of the century. Then, fashion was really only for the rich, but today we have all become women of fashion.

Social changes have had the greatest influence on how we dress. We take cheap, mass-produced clothes for granted, and feel it almost our right to change our styles and to have enough cash to do so as often and as fast as we like. 100 years ago women had to rely on sewing machines, which were few and far between. Then, Paris dominated fashion, and it took 12 years for a moderately fashion-conscious middleclass Englishwoman to catch up. At that time it was not uncommon to see clothes 20 or 30 years behind the times in remote country districts.

Fashion at the turn of the century was ostentation, a visible sign of how rich you were. Even though Queen Victoria is said to have frowned on modishness, ladies copied Queen Alexandra's frizzy fringe and dog-collar necklaces, and they wore masses of trimming on everything. Clothes were opulent and heavy and Edwardian undergarments alone weighed 10 times what ours do now. Comfort was *not* the first consideration. Rich ladies actually needed maids to lace them into their corsets and to cope with the difficulties of laundering and ironing. We know from Edwardian memoirs that a lot of hanky-panky went on, but as Cocteau said, 'to contemplate undressing a fashionable cocotte would be as complicated as under-

taking to move house.'

The ideal Edwardian woman had a matronly figure and dignified bearing. White skin was essential, rouge was considered 'fast', and any cosmetics were kept a secret. Novels of the period describe women changing up to seven times a day, but they don't reveal that one young girl in three was in

▲ *The Paris couturier Gabrielle 'Coco' Chanel, whose life story became a Broadway musical. She was the great innovator of whom Cecil Beaton said: 'She literally polevaulted women's fashions from the 19th century into the 20th.'*

domestic service with perhaps no more than a couple of dresses to her name.

The big change came with the First World War, when women went out to work in large numbers. Those who worked on the land actually found themselves in trousers for the first time.

When the war ended, there was a new craze for dancing and sport, possibly in a subconscious attempt to attract the attention of war-weary soldiers, which meant that skirts grew shorter and layers of underwear fewer. As the 20s began *Vogue* sighed: 'One cannot help wishing for a less independent, less hard, more feminine product than the average 20th-century girl.'

A fashion original

One woman emerged from this period as the embodiment of 20th-century style: Gabrielle 'Coco' Chanel. Her clothes spelled elegance and freedom—freedom of movement, freedom from ironing, freedom of self-expression. She said, 'Look for the woman in the

◄ *Greta Garbo's own style shone through all the costumes of her films, and as stars like her shot to fame Hollywood became the fashion mecca of the 30s, and its actresses fashion goddesses whose make-up and hairdos were copied by fans everywhere.*

Brigitte Bardot, Zandra Rhodes and
Jackie Kennedy: three of the top
style-setters of our time. Here Bardot
sports her famous Riviera look, an
off-the-shoulder T-shirt and shorter
than short shorts cinched at the waist
with a wide belt; Zandra Rhodes
wears an exotic creation of her own
and Jackie Kennedy looks perfectly
groomed in a simple Chanel suit.

dress. If there is no woman, there is no dress.' Chanel was the pioneer of the Total Look and the suntan and to her we owe, amongst other things, the little black dress, the cardigan suit, slingback shoes, chunky jewellery, quilted coats, grey flannel trousers with men's shirts, and above all knits, starting with the fisherman's jersey.

The 20s themselves were the years of the flapper, the woman who wanted to look slim and boyish, and not matronly or helplessly frail like her mother. The slim look necessitated far less underwear, but lots of accessories. Hair was short and bobbed to fit under the ubiquitous cloche hat.

In the 30s women began to look towards Hollywood and stars like Lombard, Dietrich, Crawford and Garbo. The silver screen presented dramatically different types of women and gave us glamour and sophistication. The fan magazine told what to do with bleached hair copied from the stars that had turned out a mess and featured a vast range of lipsticks that had been limited to light, medium and dark at the beginning of the decade. Followers of fashion now had two figureheads of style to look to and constantly switched allegiance between Paris and Hollywood.

The Second World War sent women back to work in men's jobs and the world of fashion hit another depression—clothing coupons and outfits made up out of the minimum material threw everyone back on their own resources. All that changed with a bang in 1947 at the launch of Christian Dior's New Look with its tiny waists and voluminous skirts. Suddenly femininity was ultimately desirable again and the utility and austerity of wartime looked sadly out of date.

The fashion-conscious 50s

The 50s were ultra-fashion conscious with hemlines and waistlines going up and down

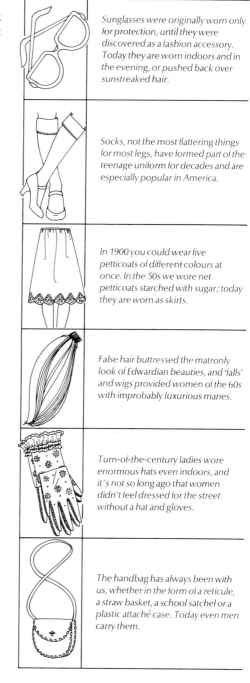

Sunglasses were originally worn only for protection, until they were discovered as a fashion accessory. Today they are worn indoors and in the evening, or pushed back over sunstreaked hair.

Socks, not the most flattering things for most legs, have formed part of the teenage uniform for decades and are especially popular in America.

In 1900 you could wear five petticoats of different colours at once. In the 50s we wore net petticoats starched with sugar; today they are worn as skirts.

False hair buttressed the matronly look of Edwardian beauties, and 'falls' and wigs provided women of the 60s with improbably luxurious manes.

Turn-of-the-century ladies wore enormous hats even indoors, and it's not so long ago that women didn't feel dressed for the street without a hat and gloves.

The handbag has always been with us, whether in the form of a reticule, a straw basket, a school satchel or a plastic attaché case. Today even men carry them.

each year as large manufacturers and multiple chainstores expanded and took their cue from Paris. This was the decade of nylon when for the first time everyone could have light, cheap underwear that would wash and dry overnight to put on clean every morning. Fastidiousness was the order of the day as the 60s dawned and the accent was on the 'right' clothes for the 'right' occasion. The figure to follow was Jackie Kennedy, and even if it wasn't true that she had her tights ironed every morning or that the word 'clothesaholic' was coined especially for her, she was rich, smart and perfectly groomed and millions of women wanted to look like her. The shops were filled with neat pillbox hats and smart boxy suits.

The other look pioneered in the 60s was swinging. Girls who were sick of emulating their mothers now had enough spare cash to find their own look, and sported ponytails, scoop necks, tiny waists, circle skirts and ballet pumps, with or without stiletto heels. The heroine was sex-kitten Brigitte Bardot; the aim was to shock. The 60s brought constant change. There were see-through crochet dresses, false eyelashes, wigs, sunglasses and tight trousers. Young people broke all the rules and at last there were young designers, such as Mary Quant, who understood them and catered for their tastes and their pockets. This was the era of the boutique.

The modern dilemma

In the 70s, clothes no longer depend on age, nor do they change with the time of day or the seasons. But what we are offered is derivative; it harks back to a distant time or place and sometimes imitates the styles we have just rejected. For some it spells freedom—for others confusion. What do you do when there is no one to follow? Today you are the star, not what you are wearing. You create your own style yourself.

Christina as a teenager in the full-skirted tight-waisted print dress typical of the mid-50s.

Two years later the hair is longer, softer, the colours strident.

Bouffant hair and chunky knits were favoured in the early 60s.

Flick-ups and an 'A'-line pinafore: Christina in the late 60s.

In the early '70s Christina looked very American with her long loose hair and tight short skirt.

Christina with her two sons. Today's look is casual and confident.

Shape up and colour in

Mercifully, today's fashions are designed for a more-or-less natural figure, but women have an astonishing ability to be any shape dictated by fashion. Edwardian women and the women of the 50s wore contraptions of great engineering skill to give them tiny waists, uplifted busts and soft feminine curves, while the 20s and the 60s called for flat, boyish figures. With effort it is possible to alter your shape, but perhaps it's your nature to accept it. Your alternatives are·to disguise what you've got or simply ignore it and wear what you please.

On the whole you shouldn't worry: what you now think of as a flaw in your figure may be high fashion next year, and anyway, the important thing is *you*.

However, there are a few ground rules for dealing with your shape when you do want camouflage, and they are easily grasped. The basic idea is to emphasize your 'good' points and cast the 'bad' ones into the background. Try on two sweaters first, one black and one white. What gives you a bigger bosom? Which gives you a bigger bottom?

Now try on a sweater that matches the colour of your jeans or skirt as nearly as possible. Do you look fatter or thinner? Add a bright red scarf at the neck or a pair of huge gold earrings and see what your eye picks out first in the whole outfit. Try the sweaters tucked in, hanging out, with loose and tight belts, with broad and narrow belts and with a belt slung on the hips.

Don't wear clothes that end at the hip if you're hippy; don't wear belts if you're fat. Clingy sweaters reveal, gentle flowing

▼ *If you were born without curves, you can afford to wear soft, full, flowing dresses with pinched waists, blouson tops and gathered sleeves.*

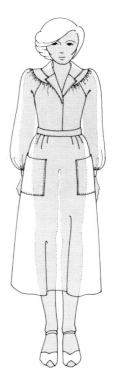

▼ *Two parallel lines are made to 'bulge' at the centre by overprinting a pattern of irradiating lines. Optical illusions created by the lines of your clothes don't always work to your advantage!*

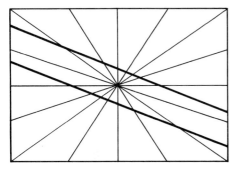

materials conceal what's underneath. A wide hemline narrows the hips; a slit up the side emphasizes your legs; vertical lines slim, horizontal ones broaden. A few well-chosen accessories can accentuate any good point, detract from any bad.

Colour can flatter or spoil your looks as much as shape. Today's colours are more subtle, more startling, more varied than ever before, but nevertheless every season the shops are swamped with a single batch of shades: muddy or clear, moody, pastel, neutral or primary, and they may or may not suit *you*.

Once upon a time there were rules for col-our: blue for blondes and pink for brunettes; redheads should never wear pink; don't mix pink and orange, don't mix blue with green; never mix patterns. Break these rules if you haven't already done so, but break them with a sense and knowledge of what colours do.

Play about a bit with colour just for fun. Start with a box of felt-tip pens and white paper. Colour a square of brilliant red and look at its reflection around the edges on the white of the paper. If that doesn't work, stare at your square for a minute and then suddenly stare at a bit of blank white paper. Your colour will have reflected its opposite

▼ *Tall thin women who don't want to emphasize their height should break up the long lean line with detail. Try waistcoats, belts, full sleeves, flowing skirts and boots that end below the hemline.*

▼ *Never draw attention to flaws in your figure. Pear-shaped women should put the focus on neck and shoulders with scarves, collars and jewellery and minimize big hips with 'A'-line skirts.*

▼ *Similarly, if you are top-heavy, you should pay more attention to your lower half. Wear full, flouncy skirts and loose sleeves to balance your shape and avoid fussy detail and loud patterns on the bust.*

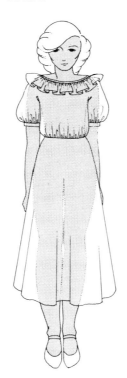

on the colour wheel—green—which is exactly how it will light your skin if you wear it next to your face. A strong colour next to your face will, of course, draw a lot of attention to itself (and away from your hips, for example), but a gentler tone of the right sort can do wonders. A light blue shirt makes your face seem even tanner in the summer than white, as it reflects up the orange tones of your tan. Bear in mind also the effect of contrast: a pale green scarf is lovely with a rosy skin, but less so if you are florid or sallow.

The colours you wear should be the colours you like as well as those that suit you, and if the colour you are crazy about is bright orange or brilliant fuchsia don't despair. Wear a becoming blue dress with an orange sash or a fuchsia brooch. Any colour can be worn in small doses. You can wear the bright colours that don't usually flatter you when you've got a good suntan, or you can try them with a white blouse underneath. If white washes you out, try cream and ivory to make you look delicate. If black washes you out, wear a collar or scarf in white, ivory or cream—something between you and your face.

Dressing in one colour can look smart and harmonious, but if it's black or a bright colour it will make your shape stand out more clearly. Dressing in shades of a colour is just as harmonious but less conspicuous.

But be warned that it is not always easy to mix shades of the same colour—blues are much harder than greens, for example. Look to the colours on either side of your main colour on the wheel·to find accompanying shades to give you harmony and a bit of

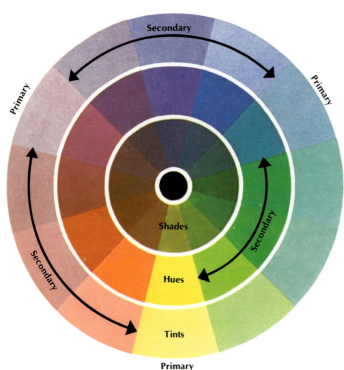

The colour wheel
In the middle ring are the clear bright hues of the primary colours. Mixed together they form the cooler secondary colours, orange, green and violet. The outer ring shows lighter tints of the six basic colours and the innermost ring is made up of the darker shades. Hues which harmonize together are those with a primary colour in common, e.g. orange, yellow, green. Contrasting hues can be found by looking directly across the wheel, e.g. red and green. Because they share no common colour their effect is vivid and exciting.

contrast. You could put blue with green or violet, for instance. Real contrasts, the colour on the opposite side of the wheel (blue's opposite is orange), can have a startling effect if they are worn in equal doses, like a sweater and skirt—but beware of overdoing it. Remember that nature uses colour contrasts in small doses (a few bright red camellias with a lot of glossy green leaves) or mixes lighter colours with dark (white lilacs amongst dark green leaves), and if you follow nature's colours you'll rarely go wrong.

If the colours you want to wear are too hectic or sallow for your complexion, try looking outwards to the border of the wheel for a lighter tint or inwards to the centre for a darker shade. You'll find that the lighter neutrals are lovely for showing off texture. Finding new colours that go together can

be difficult. It may sound mad, but try this: pile your bed high with garments of every colour you can lay your hands on. Then draw two at random. Perhaps they work together, perhaps not. Now look once more and go through all the other colours in turn until you find the one that brings your first two to life or into some kind of harmony. When you put your new colour combinations to work, remember that balance is all-important. Start with the first colour, take half as much of the second (or less) and half as much again (or less) of the third.

Colour for effect is easy to work out. Would you go for an important job interview in bright red or blue or brown? The red may give you confidence, but it could look too exciting, the blue seems confident and relaxed, the brown, they say, mature.

COLOUR SCHEMES IN CORRECT PROPORTIONS

Shades and tints of similar colour (from centre to edge of wheel)

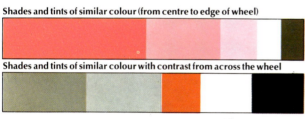

Shades and tints of similar colour with contrast from across the wheel

▼ *Which blue rectangle is largest? They're all the same size, and they illustrate how one colour appears to make another brighter and bigger, to advance or recede. Make your bottom look smaller by wearing a dark skirt and a light blouse, your bosom smaller by reversing the colours.*

Harmonious colours (next door to each other on the wheel)

Harmonious and complementary colours (opposite each other on wheel)

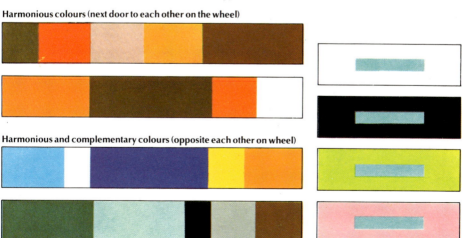

Create your own style

We wear clothes for warmth, for protection, and for modesty. And if that was all we wanted from an outfit, we could get by with a simple biblical robe to ward off the heat, the cold, the wasps and rose thorns, and to protect our modesty. But there are other quite clear reasons why we choose the clothes we wear and you need to know them to explore your own individual style.

Clothes can be worn to emphasize sex, or to make it clear that gender just isn't important. Jeans can do both, depending on whether they are skin-tight or baggy. And then there is beauty: human beings like to adorn themselves. One woman's sense of beauty will lead her to choose a dress in a glorious shade of green which, sadly, turns her face quite the wrong colour. Another will find a skirt so becoming, so glamorous, that she won't mind a bit not being able to sit down in it or how often it has to go expensively to the cleaners.

Personal taste gives psychologists a lot of clues to our personalities. A woman often uses clothing to say something about herself. She may say 'Notice me', 'I'm lonely', 'I love you', 'I'm happy', 'I'm sexy'. Every new garment she buys expresses a current mood or attitude, consciously or unconsciously.

The language of clothes

So we dress to communicate who we are, and although friends may not judge us on our appearance, strangers do. Clothes can be a sign of rebellion, and dress is said to be the commonest cause of teenagers' fights with their parents. There is also a theory that wearing ethnic clothes is a sign of the desire to embrace humanity. Some people wear

Who are you?
These questions have no correct answers, but your reactions to them will give you some insight into how you see yourself and how you dress.
1. Would you rather be Marie Antoinette or Marie Curie or Marie Osmond?
2. Have you ever been mistaken for anybody else?
3. Have you ever stayed at home because you didn't have the 'right' thing to wear?
4. When was the last time you got something in a new colour?
5. How much time does it take you to get dressed in the morning? For a party?
6. Is there a colour you hate wearing? Is there a colour you always wear?
7. Do you have a full-length mirror? A three-way mirror?
8. Are there things you feel you just can't wear because of your shape, colouring, age?
9. Would a friend agree with your description of yourself? A stranger?
10. What matters most: beauty, comfort, luxury?
11. Is it exciting to go shopping for something new?
12. What's your favourite outfit? Why? Do you wear it often or almost never?
13. Do you mind wearing the same dress to every party?
14. Do you hate to throw things away?
15. How much do you mind dog hairs on your skirt?
16. What clothes would you buy with a windfall of £5? £50? £1000?
17. Take a look at the shoes you're wearing right now? Are they scuffed?
18. Do you dress for yourself? For other women? For men? To be pretty? Sexy?
19. Do you care how you smell?
20. Is it important that clothes feel good when you touch them?
21. How do your clothes reflect your personality?
22. What would you do with a mink coat if you inherited one?
23. Does it matter to you if jewellery is real or fake?
24. How often do you buy a fashion magazine?

clothes to communicate their status, like the town-and-country shoes with the gold bits across the toes and the initial for the maker, and scarves and handbags with the designer's signature as their conspicuous feature. You might as well walk about with a sign around your neck proclaiming: 'I am an expensive lady. This handbag cost someone twice the national average weekly wage.'

Some women even assemble entire wardrobes of luxurious clothes because they believe that's the way to gain social status. Dressing for status has led to sumptuary laws, which govern such seemingly trivial things as who may wear the colour yellow or shoes with points longer than 30cm (12in). Even in our enlightened society, there are restaurants which discourage women in trousers and men without ties.

▲ Punk may not be your style, but it's unique in aiming neither to flatter the body nor to please the eye. Find your own priorities from the questionnaire.

If you are preoccupied with clothes, it may be a sign that you lack confidence in yourself. Are you forever changing your whole wardrobe just because something new is in style? Surely your own personality counts for more than what you dress it up in? Or perhaps your style never changes? This may mean that you are rigid and inflexible in other things too. Some people dress comfortably in useful, loose clothes; others' are tight, uncomfortable, high-style perhaps, but impractical. The question is: Which is you?

Are you the person you want to dress? Are you the shape you want to be? Are you

17

too fat or too thin? There is no doubt that most clothes look a thousand times better on women who are not overweight. If you are, there are three alternatives: lose weight; accept your imperfections and disguise what you can; or just ignore them and wear what you want. You can find a style that suits you whatever your size.

Really individual style doesn't come straight from the pages of a fashion magazine or from the peg of your favourite shop. Nor does it start at your head and end at your feet. It is reflected in your home environment, what you eat and how you spend your spare time. So use your feelings about the things you like best at home, your kind of music, food, flowers, everything, to work with how you look. (Although you may not want to go to the lengths of the Duchess of Windsor, who had her drawingroom painted the exact colour of her face powder.)

What's in your wardrobe?

What *is* in your wardrobe? It identifies your style and contains only what you actually

▼ *Do you recognize yourself here? Of course not. No-one is Life-of-the-Party, Miss Efficiency or Mother-of-the-Bride all week long, but it's all* *too easy to accumulate a wardrobe full of clothes that work for only one kind of occasion and spoil the look of anything else you put with them.* *Individual style emerges as you learn to mix and match. It's cheaper too!*

▶ If you really want to get the best out of your moments of relaxation, then wear something comfortable, but make sure it makes you look as good as it makes you feel. It will do wonders for your ego and others will sit up and take notice. Don't neglect your appearance when you're gardening or washing the car either. You needn't look like a frump just because you're wearing serviceable clothes. Try jeans with bibs and big pockets, coloured Wellingtons and men's shirts and jumpers.

wear—or does it? Take a long hard look at it and what it tells you about yourself. Is it tidy and can you find things when you need them? Or is it full of clothes that you mean to mend or that need constant attention and don't get it? Or high style that was out of date almost before you put it on? Or impulse buys that turned out wrong? So that in your whole wardrobe there are only a few things that you actually wear? If the answer is Yes, then give away or sell what you don't need—and give a lot of thought to what you *do*!

If you are 40 or over, chances are that your ideas about clothes were formed in the 50s or early 60s when there was really only one way to look, whether it suited you or not. You probably grew up with the idea that for each occasion, washing the car, going to a party, etc., only one kind of outfit was suitable. Today you can wear the same thing for any occasion. A well-cut boiler suit or a romantic dress in a light woollen mixture will take you anywhere. The secret is to look for things that suit *you,* whatever the occasion.

Beg, steal or borrow

Perhaps you are an individualist who hates the idea of following fashion at all. In that case you need to start off by taking a bit of time to experiment, both with your own clothes and by trying on other people's, until you find you have developed a good enough eye and feeling to pick instinctively just what will suit you. Or perhaps you are not so much concerned with being original but would like at least to appear stylish.

But how do you find out what suits you? One way to start is to copy the famous designers. Learn from the best and you'll soon see when something similar crops up at a price you can afford. You don't have to set out to be a great fashion leader to avoid being a sheep. Think back to school uniform. Everyone wore the same thing, but there was always someone who stood out from the crowd and looked better than the rest, although she might only have rolled down her socks or worn her panama tilted jauntily forward.

But as you begin to seek out your own style, don't automatically expect the shops to provide it. Try some of the ideas in the next two chapters—and the key word there is 'try'. Real individuality is not the fashion industry using you, telling you what to wear, but you using it as a storehouse of ideas, only some of which will suit you, but suit you very well. Dress sense is not a gift and can actually be learned, but it takes time and brainpower to choose your own look. However, once you know what you want and have the opportunity and the inclination to find it, you will be surprised at your own success.

You don't have to work alone adapting fashion to suit your own style. There was a time when a woman with any individuality might scorn the fashion magazines for dictating to her what she ought to wear. Now they've changed and what they give us is not *what* to wear, but *how* to wear a whole range of things, a whole series of options for all the different sorts of looks: very helpful for those of us who don't always know how to deal with new ideas, how to mix the latest fashion with what we've already got.

You should always be on the lookout for the unexpected. Don't scorn peculiar Christmas presents or well-meant hand-me-downs without at least trying them on.

One outfit—three looks
The basic outfit is neutral: a skirt and jumper in a classic, serviceable shade of beige which can be bought in any chainstore in any season. The trick is in what you do with it. **1** *The romantic adds scarves, frills and bows.* **2** *For a casually classic look add boots and a hat, woollen stockings and a toning jacket.* **3** *For an unfussy tailored look keep the lines neat, the detail small and trim. A panama trilby and high-heeled lace-ups complete the outfit. Each style is individual and easy to achieve.*

1

2

3

Style on a shoestring

Being broke will not stop you from looking good. In fact it helps if you can try to look at poverty as an asset. For one thing it concentrates the mind—or should. If you can afford to buy 20 dresses, you probably won't give them the real thought you give one dress when it's the *only* one for a long time. And listen to what the eccentric British designer Zandra Rhodes feels about people whose own special look is not derived from expensive labels but from doing the best they can without money: 'You can't define the value of what they are wearing, so their personality comes through.' Still not convinced? Think about what another expert says: 'Style is about five per cent investment and 95 per cent illusion.' So even if you've got a lot of spare cash to spend on how you look, read on, and think more about the illusion than the money.

Time is money, and for most of us taking a bit of time can really save money. If you've already given a bit of thought to how you really would like to look, and if you have taken a ruthless survey of the clothes you already have, then you will probably have arrived at another very useful principle: less is more. You do not, in fact, need *many* clothes. You need only the things you actually wear. So time spent weeding out your wardrobe is money-saving. So is the time you spend shopping, and if you want to save, that means exploring unconventional places to find your clothes. You can still get a few fantastic bargains if you look for old clothes at a jumble sale or a street market.

What to look for

Look for beautiful old materials. An Edwardian silk vest can still be found for a few pence, and it doesn't take much imagination to see it as an evening top or as a glamorous T-shirt with jeans. Look for fine workmanship and designer dresses with weights in the hem to make them hang properly. Choose things that are in good condition and reject the dresses that have been worn too often.

If you are carried away and find yourself lumbered, you won't have spent too much anyway, and you can always give, swap or sell your mistakes. It might be a good idea to join with some friends and sell off your unwanted clothes every so often, either in the privacy of your front room or on a rented stall at your local market. You're bound to at least break even. Or have a go at altering the things you've bought; by taking out the sleeves or adding a collar you could make all the difference.

There is another lesson to be learned from old clothes, a lesson that matters wherever you shop. By copying an idea from the past you can often find yourself ahead of the times. It is important to be able to recognize quality when you see it, and you can teach yourself how by looking at the workmanship of the costumes in a museum with a special collection as well as by studying the latest collections from the top designers in fashion magazines. Once you have a nodding acquaintance with The Best, you'll find yourself spotting it in the most unexpected places.

Uniform suppliers are a rich source of things to wear. You may not fancy yourself rigged out in imitation of a marine captain,

▶ *A bouquet of second-hand roses. No-one can put a price on a look like this, even though it's pieced together from attics and jumble sales.*

but think about a nurse's cape, or a sailor's middy over skinny white trousers or a pleated skirt. Once you've started thinking about the potential of uniforms and the working gear of other people for yourself it won't be long before you're trying out leotards, shepherds' smocks (lucky if you can find a real one), boiler suits and even school uniforms.

Don't pass by your local chainstores either. Use them selectively and get to know what each store does really well: perhaps tights, or scarves, or maybe good cheap shoes. If you can, visit the stores in big cities: they do have a fantastic selection compared with smaller places.. And also learn *when* to shop. Some of the big chains will re-order successful styles all season long, so there are always more coming in. Others sell out of a popular line straight away, and that's the end of that. In that case, it's best to do your shopping early in the season so that if you do find something at an amazingly low price you can get two at once (if you're *absolutely certain* you are going to need two!).

Your basic wardrobe
Everything you need for day and evening, town and country, summer and winter, can fit comfortably into one suitcase. A classic raincoat, a cord skirt, a blazer, well-cut jeans or corduroy trousers, a cotton skirt and waistcoat in an attractive Indian print,
a long-sleeved T-shirt, a silk or cotton shirt, a pair of good leather boots and a pair of strappy sandals with stacked leather heels. You might want to go for cream with navy as your main colour, or you might prefer a mixture of beiges and plum colours, but the important thing is to co-ordinate.

How to dress cheaply

1. Pick your own style and stick to it. (The danger is that it could turn out to be a bit monotonous, but you can always have fun with the things that don't cost a lot. Flower combs in your hair? Bright purple tights?)

2. Pick the colour you like and stick to it. Pale colours, beiges, greys and creams cost a bit more in laundering, but they show off cut and texture and always look expensive.

3. Minimize the number of expensive accessories. You shouldn't need many handbags. And how many pairs of shoes do you need if you've got one pair of super boots and some good sandals?

4. Buy things that do two jobs in your wardrobe. Day and night, summer and winter, outside and in, office and party—like those Indian quilted waistcoats, or little flat gold sandals which you can wear for parties, on beaches and as bedroom slippers.

5. Never buy bags or decorated scarves with makers' initials, so your style is really yours and you score over status seekers.

6. Get down to basics. What do you really need? Get your priorities right and you may find that it's worth spending that little bit extra on a cashmere polo-necked sweater because you would wear it day after day, year after year.

7. The cost per wear idea. Which is the

better buy in the long run: a £50 dress you buy because you want to look terrific at a special dance, or a £50 coat you can wear day and evening for five years? The mathematics are simple but the problem of the dance dress remains, so read on.

8. Borrow. Borrow the dress for the special dance from a friend. Chances are you won't spill lobster thermidor down the front, and anyway you've offered to pay for its dry-cleaning.

9. Make one thing your signature because you love it so much or it suits you so well. Some women have pet boots and jeans. For you, it might be a favourite shawl that you wear as often as you can.

10. When you shop be ruthless about co-ordinating colour. The jacket that goes with everything scores over the one that really only looks terrific with one skirt.

11. If you are disciplined enough, ask yourself if you really need a different outfit or look each day, or if what you really want is a uniform. Three black cashmere pullovers and three well-cut black skirts could solve your problem of what to wear to work in the winter forever!

12. If you are disciplined enough to know your needs, even if you don't quite make the uniform style your own, lash out when it comes to your own particular thing. For example, if you know that you spend the summer in T-shirts, buy half a dozen.

13. Be extravagant only in the things you need to buy anyway. If you feel like a fling after you've bought the essentials, then make it frivolous and keep it cheap. Don't buy a romantic flowered dress that you won't wear next summer when for less than a pound you can find a flower comb to wear in your hair that will say the same thing.

14. Make sure you actually have a basic wardrobe that will take you everywhere you are going over the next three months. If you haven't got one, you're likely to find yourself searching amongst your clothes for some-

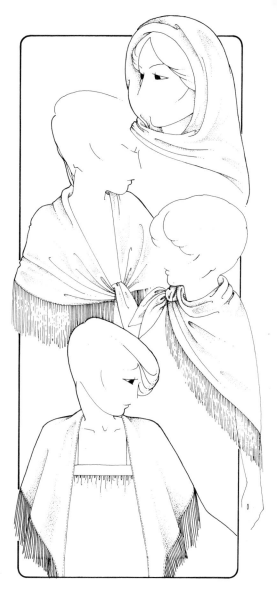

▲ If you buy a square metre of material in a light wool mixture and put a neat hem around each edge you will have made yourself a cheap and invaluable addition to your wardrobe. Choose your print carefully so that it teams with the maximum number of clothes and you'll find you never want to be without it. Wear it as a shawl draped over your shoulders; tie it outside your coat; round your waist; or follow any of the suggestions illustrated here.

thing you need very badly that simply isn't there. And then you run the risk of settling for something that's second best at twice· the price. The basic wardrobe on p.24 would dress a woman of almost any age, day and night, all year round. You might aim to have the same sort of combination in black or beige, or to replace the jeans with a navy blue needlecord skirt and the sandals with black patent court shoes.

15. Unless it gives you particular pleasure, don't reckon on spending a lot of money on a special holiday wardrobe. Instead, make sure your summer wardrobe will do for holidays as well, with some new swimwear to boost your morale. You can treat yourself when you get to your destination. You may find holidaying in France expensive, but the bright cotton espadrilles in all the French chainstores are cheap, they protect your feet from stones on the beach, and make a smashing souvenir to wear when you get home.

16. Learn to use the sales. Buy a dozen pairs of the tights you always wear. At the end of the season buy what you know you will wear next summer. Don't assume things can be altered or that you will lose weight.

You can pick up lots of fashion ideas by looking at old photographs like these, and if you're lucky you might find the garments themselves at jumble sales. The countess is wearing a beautiful riding jacket that would look stunning over a plain dress or trousers—and note the useful gadgets slung stylishly round the waist. The French sculptress shows how glamorous an overall can be, while the workman's cap and dungarees can be bought cheaply anywhere.

Either can happen, but wardrobes the length and breadth of the land are crammed with things bought on the optimist's assumption. And don't ever think that something is a bargain because it is cheaper than usual. A dress that hangs unworn in the cupboard is the most expensive one in it.

17. Re-examine your fixed ideas about what should be cheap and what should be expensive. Like shoes. Most of us grew up assuming that shoes should be the best we can afford (better fit, real leather etc.), but many smart dressers buy their shoes from chain stores.

18. This is really a chapter about choosing and buying clothes, but if you can't manage to do any real dressmaking for yourself, at least contemplate what you can do with a minimum of skill. Take a big square of cotton or one of those light woollen mixtures and hem it. Then, have a go at seeing how many different ways you can wear it.

19. When you see exactly what you want at the right price, don't dither, buy it then and there. .

20. When you spend money, make sure you get something that's beautiful in itself as well as useful to your wardrobe.

21. Don't waste any more money than you need to on hairdos and make-up (see pp. 56-9).

22. Save money and look better at the same time. Give up smoking. Give up buying spirits and stick to orange juice and wine. Give up your lunch hour and go to a yoga class instead.

23. Make the most of the things you've got. But that's a chapter in itself.

▶ Why not widen your horizons and look for your fashion accessories in uniform suppliers', specialist sports shops, cheap chainstores, or second-hand markets? One good find could give you the inspiration for a whole new look.

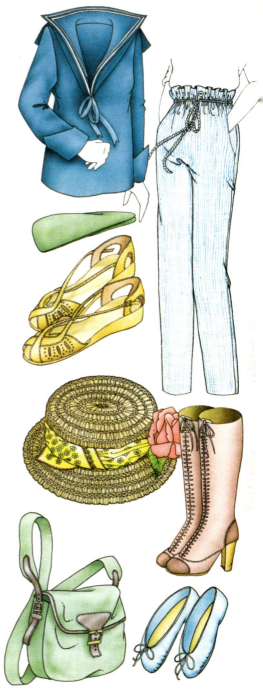

Make your clothes work for you

Were you brought up to believe that you have to suffer to be beautiful? Or perhaps experience has convinced you that there is no true style when you are uncomfortable in what you are wearing. Women have an astounding track record of wearing things that are not merely uncomfortable in order to keep up with fashion, but downright

▼ *Would you suffer for fashion? Women always have done. Corsets are still with us, though they may not be so tight, but what about stiletto heels, pencil skirts, platform shoes—and punk?*

crippling, dangerous or unhealthy. Today, except perhaps for the punk bondage clothes, most of our fashion is fairly comfortable and easy to wear, although doctors do warn us of the risks of wearing too-tight jeans and tights: thrush is one of them.

Now look at comfort from the other point of view: that of positively seeking it out. For example, if you stand and walk a lot, why not adopt support-stockings or tights? You can find them in a much greater range of colours these days, and if you can't find the colour you really want, it's not hard to wear a lighter shade and put on another pair of ordinary tights, darker, brighter or patterned, over it. What's more, two pairs of tights worn together are warmer.

If you sweat a lot, look for natural fabrics rather than the man-made ones. If you are a shivery sort of person, find pretty little vests and wear them all winter. If what you like to wear never seems to have pockets, make or buy one (or two) on a belt round the waist, like the latest ones from Paris. The thing to do is not to let your need for comfort fight against your sense of style, but to let comfort serve your own personal style.

Make the most of what you've got

Wartime children grew up with the rhyme, 'use it up, wear it out, make it do or do without', and 30 years later in the penniless 70s it's still good advice. So here are some basic tips to double the use of what you've already got in the wardrobe.

1. Take a look at what you've got and decide what you're going to do with it. You can simply put old things away for a while. Most clothes do come back into style sooner or later, usually in a quite different form. Or you

can give away what you don't want, and start off a new uncluttered woman.

2. Revamp what you might otherwise give away. Spray a pair of scuffed boots gold. Dye faded bras and pants a lovely coffee colour with cold tea.

3. Keep a box or a drawer for interesting ideas and bits: things like buttons, ribbons, lace, an old apron with good pockets, a dress that would cut down to a blouse. The things themselves will give you ideas for changing old clothes.

4. Learn to add and subtract. Just because a dress came to you with a belt, you are not compelled to wear it like that. And if you hate the nasty plastic button on an otherwise handsome jacket, replace it with a genuine bone button. Bone buttons are expensive, but they look it.

5. See the potential in everything. That's how a lot of today's fashion has been arrived at. Examples? Men's bow ties, huge men's shirts, Edwardian petticoats, boiler suits.

6. Learn to sew, knit, crochet, embroider, dye etc. Really worth the effort if it frees you from shop prices and means you can rework both your own things and jumble bargains to create something fantastic.

7. Organize a couple of automatic outfits. Say, something for when you are feeling the blues and can't be bothered, and something that you always feel festive in for a night out.

8. Lend, and for that matter give, freely to trusted friends. For one thing they will lend and give freely to you, with any luck. And for another, it gives you a chance to see an old familiar outfit in a new light.

9. Be more fastidious. We all know what the combination of a grey flannel skirt that ought to have gone to the cleaner's two wearings ago with a blouse that's a bit grey about the cuffs looks like. If you've got plenty of odd buttons, it's easy to replace a missing one straight away. If you learn how to iron properly you will not only look crisper, you

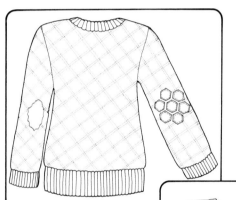

Never throw away a favourite jumper because it's worn away at the elbow or cuff. There are several ways to give it a new lease of life. Make a decorative patch for the elbow (above).

Turn up the sleeve and make a chunky cuff. Looks even better with decorative stitching on cuffs and ribbing.

Add lace or broderie anglaise to ragged cuffs, and to finish off sew a matching 'collar' at the neck.

might even find you enjoy it more; and you'll save money if you can deal with a silk shirt yourself instead of sending it to the dry-cleaner. Don't pray the ladder in your tights won't show—put on fresh ones. If your skirts aren't lined, get a woven, silk or rayon petticoat. Take your shoes to the mender's *before* the heels wear down.

10. See all your clothes differently, other people's too for that matter. Don't shun the outrageous; you may find a little goes a long way, especially if you mix it with things that seem a bit dull or outworn. Don't, for example, regard those spike-heeled red patent leather ankle boots as a mistake until you have taken a look at them with a grey flannel suit, or a peasant skirt, or your skinniest jeans.

11. Eliminate the distinction between day and evening clothes. A pair of rust satin or velvet trousers will take you through 24 hours. So will a highwayman's shirt.

12. Eliminate the distinction between the seasons. Take skirts: there are light wool and cotton mixtures in lovely flower prints that are almost never too hot or too cold, especially if you choose one that will go with T-shirts in the summer and polo-necked sweaters in the winter.

13. Think in layers. That's no longer new advice, but some people have trouble carrying it out. For example, don't fret that you can't afford a new winter coat. Work out the layers you need to keep warm. A light raincoat to wear over your blazer? A quilted waistcoat to wear under your classic rain-coat? A huge woolly scarf?

14. Wear things differently. Don't stop at a satin jacket over tweed trousers, but wear things that belong on the outside inside, and vice versa. Wear a shirt as a jacket; wear two shirts at once. Wear a slim jacket belted without anything underneath. Wear a V-necked sweater two sizes too large. Wear a cardigan buttoned up instead of open. Wear things too big, too small, too old (try half-glasses in tortoiseshell), too young (school aertex shirts).

15. Learn to mix. That's the real story of style in the 70s. It comes with practice and costs you nothing because you start off with what you've already got. Begin on a free afternoon with some good music on the radio and your full-length mirror in front of you. (A full-length mirror is essential. It saves a lot of money and agony when you know what you actually look like.) Lay out all your clothes on the bed in categories, then just go ahead and try everything on with everything else and count up the number of new outfits you emerge with. Mix your oldest clothes with your newest. Mix tweeds with satin and lace. Mix country clothes with city, day clothes with night. Mix the classic look with the romantic to achieve the now familiar combination of a blazer over a lacy petti-coat dress. Mix the masculine with the feminine: a grey flannel suit with slinky black stockings and soot-black, tarty high heels.

Modern times

Mixing is really not the easiest thing to learn, but remember it's your own mix you are after and whatever you come up with in your experimenting is free. As you take a look at some of the prevailing themes of style you will see how much of each has been arrived at in exactly this way.

▶ *Diane Keaton and Woody Allen in* Annie Hall. *Keaton, Best-dressed Woman of 1978, Best Actress of 1978, appears in her own clothes in the award-winning film. A pioneer of the Mix-it Look, she epitomizes the fashion message of today and is copied by millions.*

Modern classics

Classic clothes get their name because they don't date and can be worn with confidence from year to year.

The clothes and accessories of the classic look on these pages all have several things in common. They are understated for the woman who doesn't want to stand out in a crowd. They suit women of all ages and on the whole they go with everything. They combine comfort and elegance, practicality and dash. Skirts, trousers and boots allow for movement; bags are of real leather and last for years; coats, shirts, pullovers and jackets are soft, loose, and often belted.

One of the most eyecatching features of the classic look is its hats. The epitome of good sense and good style, they range from berets through panamas and boaters to trilbys and soft floppy wide-brimmed affairs for summer. Each has a purpose: to shield the wearer from the sun, wind or rain, or to keep the hair in place, but the charm of the hat lies greatly in the way you wear it: the way you tilt the brim up or down, pull a beret jauntily to one side—maybe

with a brooch pinned above the ear—or pull the whole hat forwards so that your eyes are cast into a mysterious shadow.

Classic materials are natural fibres and leather, and because they last for years they are worth spending as much money on as you can afford. Look for silk, cashmere, woollen knits and pure wool tweeds, linen, grey flannel and fine cotton. However, some of today's man-made fibres look almost as good as the real thing and cost half the price. The same goes for jewellery. Real pearls, precious stones, cameos and heavy gold chains and bangles are ideal with this look, but if these are beyond your means, then keep your eye open for other real ornaments

like ivory, wooden or china beads, or old-fashioned painted or feather brooches. That way at least your jewellery won't be identifiable as coming from a particular chainstore.

Quality of cut is just as important as quality of material in classic clothes, and you should aim for simple, uncluttered lines

and fine workmanship. Cream, grey, black, white, fawn and navy are the basic classic colours, and these go well with clear reds, blues, greens and yellows. But don't be rigid in your colour choice: the classic look will take virtually any colours, although sugary pastels and fussy patterns should be used with care, if at all.

Classic clothes that have been with us for years are familiar to everyone. They include regulation raincoats and school coats, camelhair coats, pullovers in shetland, lambswool and cashmere, ribbed stockings, silk shirts and headscarves, twinsets, grey flannel suits and simple button-through shirt-waister dresses. But the list is growing all the time, and amongst the more recent classics are jeans, T-shirts, kaftans, and a multitude of easy lacey knits.

The classic look

The classic look means never having to say you're sorry, you're not dressed 'right'. Classic clothes are simple—the basics of any wardrobe, and are neutral enough to be dressed up differently for every occasion. They are practical, they are elegant, they are timeless and ageless. The whole look puts itself together effortlessly.

But there are pitfalls. If you don't use your imagination you can look dull and if you stick to the look too rigidly it can dim your eyes to new ideas. It can look dowdy if its components are of inferior materials or shoddy workmanship. It can be ageing, and while you don't need to spend your entire life looking after clothes of good quality, it's easy to ruin the effect if you're not fairly fastidious. Above all, it can be monotonous, for you as well as for the beholder, as monotonous as wearing the same scent for years without experimenting.

To make the classic look pay its way and be worth the effort you need to keep an open mind and use your imagination with other more frivolous items in your wardrobe. To liven up your grey polo-necked pullover and pleated skirt, try a brightly patterned quilted jacket. Wear bright yellow or fuchsia espadrilles (another new classic) or very high, strappy gold kid sandals with a plain button-through dress. Wear the laciest romantic blouse you can find with your old tweed suit, or a gold lurex jersey, or a bright green silky T-shirt.

And remember that it's not just the clothes that make up your look. The simple hairstyles and natural cosmetics traditionally held to be classic can produce too much of a muchness, so if the rest of you is going to be inconspicuous, play about with your make-up, wear your hair in a *coupe sauvage* or an Afro-frizz, pin it back with a jewelled butterfly to keep it out of your face, or push it under a sophisticated turban.

A.Knok

New romantics

The romantic look is always with us, but never more so than now. For some women it's a beauty treatment, for others a disguise. For some it means looking pretty and fragile, for others it means a nostalgia for the past or a reaching out towards the romantic East or the gypsy life. Practicality is not the first thing romantic women look for in their dress, nor is simplicity—you can be as cluttered as you like.

But because it can be an exaggerated look, it takes a bit of putting together. The bits and pieces that add to that air of gentle, innocent femininity include pretty shoes: girlish shoes, ballet slippers, pretty sandals, high-style boots in pale, impractical colours. Handbags are straw baskets, cane boxes, reticules, beaded evening bags from the attic. Hats are flower-trimmed boaters of coquettish, floppy straw with wide brims and veiling. Lace is everywhere —blouses, collars and cuffs, scarves and handkerchiefs, and above all on petticoats—and so are embroidery, ribbons, bows and flowers. Shawls go with all the different romantic looks: the lacey knits, dramatic gypsy black with roses, and, if you can find them, Victorian paisley and cashmeres.

The new romantics wear cameo brooches, sashes to show off their waists (or scarves bound as sashes). They wear capes, cloaks, boleros, pochettes on strings, and often as many of these things as possible.

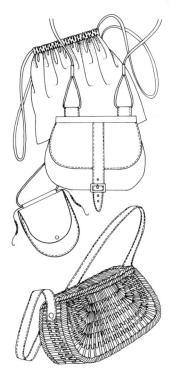

Romantic colours are soft pastels, often mixed together, and romantic prints are flower gardens. The fabrics are real ones, and they are soft and crushable: silk, cotton, velvet, soft lace, chiffon. The hothouse look means soft and lacey feminine underwear — mercifully now abundant in easy-care, man-made fabrics in the chain-stores, and nightgowns, not pyjamas.

And it can mean wearing underwear as outerwear. We've got used to seeing those Edwardian camisoles and petticoats worn as summer dresses. The second-hand prices have shot up, but the mass manufacturers were quick to provide the shops with new 'old' clothes. Until the prices went up, jumble,

rummage, attics and second-hand shops were the great source for the gentle, embroidered and lace-trimmed nightgowns that a daring new romantic can wear today as evening dress.

The exotic romatic came into her own in the 60s when hippies and pop stars followed the dress of the Middle and Far East with kaftans, cheong sams, peasant sandals, embroidered Chinese robes, jackets and skirts.

A romantic affair

Most romantic clothes are more suitable for everyday wear. A good idea is to mix the masculine and feminine elements in one outfit as they are mixed in our own personalities: lacey tights (if they are too pale they'll make your legs look fatter) with a plain skirt, ballet slippers with men's trousers (Garbo did it), a cobweb pink woollen scarf with a tweed coat, or frilly knickers under a tailored skirt. Or flowers everywhere.

If you know yourself well enough to know that the full-blown romantic look is you, if you've felt starved for really pretty things until quite recently and if you think you'll go on wanting them, then now is the time for you to contemplate spending a bit more on clothes than you usually do, because the reaction to the plethora of heavy, fussy, frivolous femininity is underway, and it might be a good idea to stock up.

The ultimate in romantic clothes are a feast for the eye. They can make you feel and even move quite differently, but take care not to go overboard in case you find the clothes wearing you instead of the other

way around. Romantic dresses are tight-waisted and full-skirted, or loose smocks. They have ruffles, full sleeves, round necks, and flowing, curved lines, not straight ones. The prettiest dresses are a beauty treatment in themselves, and they do not demand any exaggerated grooming, just your own natural hair, as messy as you like if it's curly, and enough make-up to make sure you can look gentle without being overpowering. Because the lines are soft and gentle, they will suit you if you are overweight, and many women with a weight problem have lovely shoulders for the off-the-shoulder styles.

The romantic look is for spectator sports, for summer even more than for winter, for the clean country air more than for cities.

Menswear

The 60s gave us clothes labelled unisex as if the idea of dressing like a man were something new. The truth is that even before Chanel we were borrowing from the opposite sex—think of tailored Edwardian riding habits, and how quick we were to latch on to trousers for sports. Now every woman wears something that started with men—a whole range of bits and pieces styled and tailored for our rather different shapes. All sweaters started as male working gear (fishermen's jerseys, for example) or sports clothes, like T-shirts. Think of those men's golf cardigans and knitted waistcoats, long and soft and comfortable, and of fair isle pullovers like the ones the Prince of Wales made popular in the 30s. Women have now adopted tailored shirts, the collarless ones as well, and all kinds of jackets and trousers from blue jeans and corduroys to cavalry twill and velvet or satin.

Lately we have seen more men's clothes in their natural state. In the 50s American teenagers borrowed their father's shirts to wear outside their jeans, and we learned how fragile and feminine a woman can look in something that is frankly too big and too masculine. London today is full of women in men's tweed jackets worn much too big, and we've actually reached the point now where they are designed and manufactured too big. A warning: it's a look that's best if the materials are soft or the jacket is unlined. And if you try it, experiment with pushing the sleeves up a bit. .

It's worth extending the choice of places where you buy clothes to include men's suits, coats, jackets, shirts and trousers if you are tall enough and if your figure is fairly straight up and down. Try on V-necked sweaters and round-collared shetlands that are too big or too small and see which suits you best. If you are smaller, perhaps with more curves, you could always look to the boy's departments. The women who do dress in men's and boy's clothes claim that they are better made and harder-wearing than the female copies.

Masculine accessories, like boots, moccasins and loafers, add to the look. And it might be worth seeing if you could find a pair of boy's flat patent leather dancing pumps or pageboy wedding shoes. Workmen's caps have become high fashion, and no style lasts like a velours or panama trilby. Look for men's cashmere and silk evening scarves too, and if you dare, you might experiment with a

pair of men's cream silk pyjamas for a bit of evening glamour with comfort.

And why not try their dressing gowns: huge towelling robes for the bath, paisley silk or man-made Nöel-Cowardish lounging robes over a black polo-necked sweater and black velvet trousers. You might even find that one of those chainstore velvety velours dressing gowns for men makes a cozy evening coat.

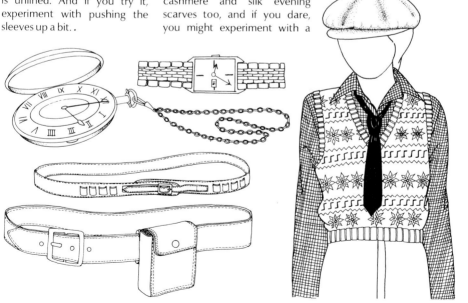

Why can't a woman dress more like a man?

One of the greatest advantages of the masculine look is that it's very easy to organize at its simplest: a suit, a shirt (or a Lord Fauntleroy ruffled blouse?), a pullover, practically any shoes except court shoes, a shoulder bag. You can top it all with a cap—or strike a contrast with huge flower earrings. You can tie a lace shawl around your shoulders or wear a foulard tie high on the neck above an open collar.

You can follow the lead of Diane Keaton (p.31) by teaming your flowered flouncy skirt with a man-tailored shirt and a blazer. And without going to extremes, you can even find a certain female glamour in a man's suit (or at least a suit tailored to look like a man's) in a pale beige or cream and worn very simply, perhaps with its own tight waistcoat and nothing more than a pair of very high-heeled sandals to extend the long, lean look.

You can wear your hair as it falls and forget about make-up (just enjoy a boyish freedom), or if that seems too masculine and drab you can remind your audience of your femininity with as gentle or wild hair and make-up as you like.

There are disadvantages. Trousers, especially men's, can look awful on some bottoms. We are longer from crotch to waist than men, and a tight waist on trousers can emphasize hips too much, though hipsters are often the answer for women with womanly shapes. A masculine look can be too harsh on some women, and ageing on others, so you need to take a good look at yourself. But the current vogue for men's things has expanded our choice not only in the shops but as second-hand sales and in the wardrobes of husbands, brothers, and boyfriends. Dressing like a man is one way to forget fashion and embrace comfort, but be ready for jokes if you go too far.

A.Kwok

The sporty look has always been with us, but it is only very recently that it has been considered as fashionable. It is a daytime look, unless you choose to take the advice of one glossy fashion magazine which once suggested trying a track suit, perhaps with high-heeled gold sandals, for evening parties. It is also an outdoor look that doesn't mean you have to shiver to look good. And it's great virtue is comfort. The clothes that people wear for serious sport have to be clothes that they can actually move in, so they are perfect for the woman who places comfort above suffering to look good. If you are discriminating they also stand up to hard wear and the weather. New, man-made fabrics mean jackets you can just throw into a washing machine and forget about ironing, colours that should not run or fade, and materials that dry quickly. Think, for example, about the kind of shirt a football player needs on a day when it is showery one minute and sunny the next: quick-drying nylon, not soggy cotton.

The bits and pieces that make up the look also put the accent on comfort. Low golfing shoes (get the spikes removed!), tough boots, like climbing boots that keep your feet comfortable all day with ridged rubber or crepe soles, now come in a huge range of bright colours. Think also of tennis shoes and trainer shoes. And you can wear golf caps and fishing hats to go with them, and finish off your outfit with a big practical watch. A lot of the most stylish handbags in the shops at the moment also derive from sport, from the

practical needs of the men who go huntin', shootin' and fishin', like grouse- and fishing-bags with nets for your catch (or your shopping). Or you can go straight to the shops that sell the real thing to look for a proper canvas and leather cartridge bag that should last for years.

Sailors', skiers' and campers' anoraks have now become fashion garments. The ones made out of a thin nylon skin are designed to be light-weight and are easily stuffed into a bag or pocket on showery, windy days. The quilted ones give perfect protection in cold weather and now you can also get them in pastel colours as well as bright

ones. Along the same lines there are jockeys' jackets and the stock-necked shirts of dressage riders, not to mention the quilted nylon 'husky' jackets and waistcoats the horsey set prefer. If you do a lot of bad-weather walking, a rubberized riding raincoat might be exactly what you need, but remember that they tend to get a bit hot.

A woman with a sporty style and a practical mind will also look for driving gloves, golf gloves, visors and sunglasses. High fashion is also beginning to turn to those figure-hugging racing swimsuits that help champion swimmers to glide through the water fast, as a sexy alternative to bikinis.

Spectator sports

You can see the influence of sports clothes in drawstring waists on blouses, jackets and trousers. But the real story of the sporty look is a wardrobe full of tops and bottoms, trousers, not skirts. Polo-necked sweaters did start off on the polo field, and we've now accepted cricket sweaters, tennis shirts, striped rugby jerseys, hooded sweatshirts, and baseball jackets. Then there are all the jeans and corduroy trousers, and jodhpurs. And track suits. And perhaps you remember how the stretch trousers developed for skiing in the early 60s were suddenly worn everywhere.

You may not harbour a secret fantasy of boxing a round with Muhammed Ali, but if you've got long, lean legs and are young enough, think how super a pair of boxing shorts would look on the beach. You may never go on safari either, but we've seen

safari-style suits around for so long now that we've forgotten their sporting origin. A good safari jacket ought to be long enough to flatter your bottom, look just as good with a skirt as with trousers, and if you like the feel and the convenience of pockets, why not make one up in satin or velvet for special occasions?

Try lumberjacks' jackets, oiled fishermen's jerseys, mountaineers' socks worn outside your trousers in sneakers or tucked over boots; skiing balaclavers (with only your eyes showing you'll keep warm and look alluring!). Sherlock Holmes hats in fur and tweed are dashing and protective in bad weather, and for summer, if you're lucky enough you might be able to pick up sixth-formers' sports clothes at jumble sales.

Sports clothes don't date rapidly, and you needn't worry about your hair or make-up. Today you can wear them almost every-where and look good.

Glamour

You don't have to be beautiful to look glamorous. If you take it seriously (and unless your sort of glamour has a touch of the sluttish, it's one look that seems to lack a sense of humour), you can be as plain as you like and choose the rich or elegantly simple clothes that go with careful dramatic make-up. It helps if you've already got striking features, and it is one look where black and brown women start off with a distinct advantage.

With glamour, the whole is greater than the sum of its parts, and the look depends on its wearer. Close your eyes and think of Marlene Dietrich on stage: comfort and practicality don't seem to play as much of a role in her appearance, as the dramatic, larger-than-life effect. If it's glamour you're looking for, you've got to work it out very carefully, because perfect grooming doesn't come about by accident.

Start with your underwear. Suspenders and stockings look and feel terrifically sexy, tights don't. Throw away or dye discoloured white undies and replace them with dramatic black. Think in terms of texture and go for soft, slinky, clinging fabrics like silk—or nylon!

The high life

Glamour is very personal. Perhaps a good deal of your life is efficient and hardworking, with a wardrobe built for the purpose, but when you want to express the part of you that is most alluringly sexy and feminine, one super dress gives you the chance. If you know that you look absolutely stunning in it, there is no reason not to wear it forever, because it will always be your own look, even if it is a bit eccentric or not conventionally in style at the moment. And there are certain dresses that confer instant glamour, like the exotic, diaphanous, glittery evening gowns that have made Thea Porter famous all over the world, or Yuki's cunningly draped jerseys. Their styles have been copied cheaply, and with a great deal of luck you might even find a genuine original second-hand.

Daytime glamour is harder to picture. Most women don't live lives that can accommodate it, but think of the effect of a cream silk shirt with pale cream trousers, perhaps with a man's cream silk scarf and a camelhair coat (it doesn't have to be blonde mink) and pale boots. Impractical? That's one of the disadvantages, but there are cream shirts in man-made fibres that look as good as silk and leather dyes with which you can retouch pale boots when they get grubby or scuffed.

To look glamorous, it's almost a neccessity to be thin, and to wear high heels, shoes that you might be able to dance in, but scarcely work in or walk further than the nearest limousine. Shoes, like the rest of the wardrobe, should shine or give off a richness, whether they are black patent leather thigh boots or strappy gold or silver sandals. There's no doubt that shoes can be very sexy, and sandals, mules and transparent plastic effectively give the intriguing half-undressed look that complements glamorous fabrics so well.

Anything goes

Now that the old rules are gone, anything goes—at least for a trial run. You can aim to achieve the look of someone who has thrown anything on without looking, or you can seek exquisite perfection and simplicity with a white T-shirt and white trousers. You can dress for fun without bothering about whether you look 'right', you can wear every fad that comes along without caring if it's becoming, you can wear fancy dress from dawn until midnight or later. It depends on how conspicuous you want to be, if you don't mind being stared at or if you positively want to shock. You can race to be the first with something new and lead the fashion or dress as eccentrically

as you like without worrying if you find followers or not. And if you don't wish to do any of those things, you can use the bright ideas and fancies that always seem to suit someone else to give a lift to your own, more conventional tastes.

Think of all the jokey accessories that are everywhere now and what they would do for your old standbys. When you forget about flattery you can have a lot of fun with feet and legs. Wear bright red wellington boots, yellow track shoes, brilliant blue plastic sandals. Wear leg warmers in rainbow stripes, wear sunshine yellow or magenta tights. Wear huge, baggy sweaters in shocking colours over tights, or tight trousers; wear shorts or bloomers as if they were skirts. Carry a vinyl shoulder bag that is made to look like the yellow carton a roll of film comes in, or a pink nylon miniature duffle bag instead of decent but rather dull brown leather. Try bright little woolly caps with your most inconspicuous old coat. Wear anything you like on a cord around your neck—wear a dozen cords dangling with things if your neck is strong enough. Wear a whistle on the dance floor and blow it when you feel the urge. Carry a striped golf umbrella—it might be harder to lose it if it's easier to spot.

If you know that you can't carry off an entirely comical look and don't want to, play about with all the advertising T-shirts. The outrageous look suits the young best, and it gives teenagers a thousand different ways to follow the crowd and learn their own style at the same time. So take a fresh look at your children and grandchildren or the junior in the office and see how their lack of cash and inhibitions can offer you a bit of sparklé. You may not imitate the early punk style of dressing in garbage bin liners, but think of it as imaginative style on the cheap.

The punk styles may seem aggressive to you, but what's wrong with dressing aggressively if that's how you feel. And if a designer like Zandra Rhodes can accept holes, bathplug chains and safety pins as legitimate decoration on a dress, you can learn to see anything as potential trimming too.

Make mistakes, make them cheaply if you can, and learn from them.

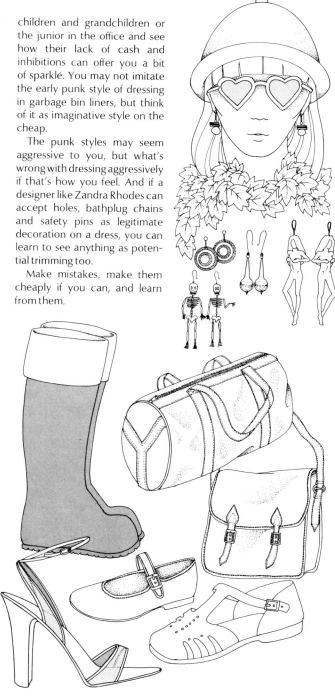

Instant fashion

Play about with the frankly fake, with fluorescent socks, transparent plastic belts or belts with a message. Wear a nylon leopard-printed catsuit if you dare—or try the print as a T-shirt or knickers if you don't dare. Wear the colour you like where you like, whatever the effect. Try out everything that seems odd to you in your own wardrobe, odd clothes, odd colours, odd combinations. You've nothing to lose—if you don't like it, you don't have to wear it. After all there was a time when blue jeans were thought a bit peculiar.

The disadvantages of all this experimenting include being stared at. Artifice usually means a bit of effort. Outrageous clothes are often throwaway buys which are quick to fall apart and prove expensive in the long run if you have to keep replacing them or you can't face wearing them after all. They also date quickly and you may not want to look out of fashion. On the other hand they are fun, they are cheap, they give you the freedom to do as you like, and the lessons they teach can help you brighten up your own basic style.

Finishing touches

There's never been a time when most of us could change our hair and make-up as freely as we can now. Our looks are other people's big business, and the manufacturers offer a huge range of products. Anything goes, and the only problem is to work out just what you want from your hairdo. Lately, the trend has been towards hair that doesn't need too much attention—and there's been a corresponding increase in the number of products people want us to buy as we pay fewer and fewer visits to the salon.

And when you do visit him, make the most of your hairdresser. Your first priority should be honesty. It does you no good if you don't admit that your hair is permed or dyed. And don't expect your hairdresser to guess what you want in the way of a new cut. Take a picture or two along to show him. And then take his or her advice when you are told that the particular style won't suit your hair.

If you want to save time and money, find a style that needs cutting only once every six weeks. Have one of the new perms that doesn't need setting and grows out gently into a softer style, saving you every second perm. Investigate the new style of tinting in three or four colours, which grows out naturally without the roots needing to be redone frequently.

Many women have discovered the ease of the new frizzy but gentle perms: it's OK these days to look as if you've been dragged

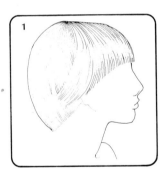

If you hate spending time on your hairstyle, spend money on a really professional short cut instead: wash it and leave it to dry. You can't miss and it'll suit anything from punk to classic. (**1**)

If you like your hair longer, softer, it'll need more attention. Get a professional cut and beware split ends, greasy roots. You may want to spend a few minutes curling the ends. (**2**)

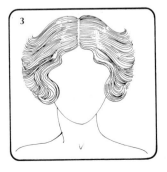

Devote a little time to your hair and you can have a romantic soft wave. If you have fine or wayward hair a soft perm would be advisable, but blow-drying is essential. (**3**)

If you want a more elaborate style, you will need to spend quite a lot of time caring for your hair, unless it falls naturally into the curls you like. Consult your hairdresser. (**4**)

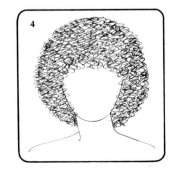

through a hedge backwards, with either romantic tangles or a savage mess to show for it. And all you need to do each morning is to spray a little water on it and run your fingers through it.

And a word about shampooing: There is no one answer to the question: How often? Here are two hints. If you have the courage to keep letting your hair get quite dirty and greasy before you wash it, you may find that you can gradually increase the intervals between washing, as the natural oils take longer to appear. Also, if you really do feel you need to wash your hair often, remember it is the rinsing that gets it clean, not the amount of shampoo. So use only a little shampoo and rinse twice as well as you ever have before.

If you want to change your hair with minimum fuss and expense for a special occasion, don't forget how much fun you had experimenting with it as a teenager. If you have straight, even hair, try plaiting it wet into as many little plaits as you like and letting it dry into fairy-tale princess ripples. Or use a bit of imagination with ornaments. If you find yourself wearing the same dress to every party, you can often ring the changes effectively with a different kind of bow or flower comb in your hair. It's a great lesson to see how fashion designers use hair ornaments or head-dresses as part of a total style.

Make-up

The experts claim that women are less aware of changes in make-up styles than in hair and clothes and that an out-of-date face is even more ageing than the same old wardrobe. We've been through powder to take the shine off the face and gleamers to put it back on again, through flat, almost white lips and glossy red ones, and some women still cling to their false lashes. Today you can be pale or tan, you can look as

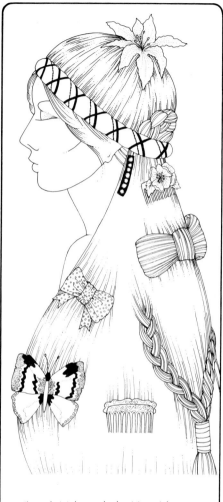

If your hair is long, whether it is straight or curly, fine or thick, you may like to add combs, bows, plaits, hairpins or even chopsticks to change your look from time to time. Here are a few ideas to copy. Hair ornaments feature largely in almost every fashion show, and if you want to create your own look from head to toe, you shouldn't be afraid to use them—and they are very cheap.

natural as you like—or as wild.

To find your own look, ask yourself the kind of questions you ask about your clothes and your hair. How much effort do you really want to make? How much money do you want to spend? Do you use make-up to feel good, to make yourself beautiful, to alter your looks or as a form of decoration?

One thing all the experts would agree on, whatever your answers: your health shows in your face. So if you never get enough sleep, if you drink or smoke too much, if you never eat enough fresh fruit and vegetables, don't expect make-up to do it all for you. And remember you must always start off with a clean face and some kind of moisturizer.

There are two ways of looking at make-up. You can either just put yourself and a lot of money in the hands of an expensive shop or salon who will show you what suits you and sell you what they can, or, if like most women you're short of cash, you can start by really noticing other faces, especially the women who look good to you in magazines and on television. Notice first of all the things that don't cost money. For example: are eyebrows thick or thin, what shape are the lips, is the eyeliner being worn inside the lower lid as well as the upper, do the eyes get all the attention or is it divided between eyes and mouth, is the blusher or rouge used for colour or shaping, or both? Magazines are invaluable when it comes to make-up because they give you actual step-by-step instructions without insisting on a particular brand of cosmetics.

Now experiment. Before you start buying cosmetics, have a look at what you've already got—most of us hoard drawers full of old lipsticks and eye shadows. Models today are getting much subtler effects by mixing colours, and if you've got the brushes, you can try the same technique to get new life out of old colours. Mix them together either in the pot or right on your lids or lips, perhaps adding a layer of gloss

▲ *Your summer tan stays natural with moisturizer and just a touch of lip and eye gloss.*

on top. (Margaret, Duchess of Argyll, is said to use vaseline to give her eyelids a shine.) You may find that a mix actually suits you better than a particular colour, although you probably won't want to go to the lengths of one of London's top make-up artists who commonly wears 10 colours on her eyelids, subtly blended of course.

When it comes to buying new cosmetics, have courage and don't let yourself be dictated to by the cosmetic houses. Remember always that the advertisers are operating on the theory that they can sell you a dream of fantasy beauty—and you are a real person with a real face. No make-up ever devised will ever make you as pretty as when you smile with real delight. You do not have to buy a range of toning lip, nail and

▲ *Warm-looking tawny reds and browns look bold and confident in winter.*

▲ *Dramatize your eyes for evening and add shape to your cheekbones with blusher.*

eye colours to be beautiful, and you ought to have a chance to try stuff on before you buy. You may think the 'testers' in the stores are unhygienic, but they do give a better idea of colour than smearing foundation or lipstick on the back of your hand and getting home and finding that you've brought quite the wrong shade.

Remember too that the most expensive is not always the best. You may find that you need to spend money on a good foundation, but that a cheap cleansing lotion or moisturizer is all you need, especially if your skin is young or oily or both. And don't bother to buy expensive lipsticks and eye shadows: it's far more exciting to have a larger range of cheaper products so that you can experiment with a new look as often as you want

to. And it's not a bad idea to start off by exaggerating with colour and line—it'll teach you your limits and you can always tone it down to suit your face.

A last word about those so-called worst features: forget them. Most of us worry too much about tiny imperfections: the very things that give us character. Disguise just draws attention to wrinkles and bags, and the cleverest thing to do is to distract the eye to another part of the face, perhaps with an exotic shade of lipstick. It feels wonderful if you can just plain break the habit of, for example, hiding your ears because someone once pointed out that they stick out, and put on a pair of big flowered earrings for the first time. Try it and see.

Style at any age

In the 50s, girls of 17 tried to look like women of 35. In the 60s women of 35 tried to look like girls of 17, In the 70s women can choose any look they fancy, and finding your own style no longer has to do with what age you are. If you are 50 or older the great trick now is to forget that there used to be rules. And remember that you've got one great advantage over younger women: your age; or rather the fact that by 40 you have developed a style of your own. Remember your own teens, or look at the teenagers to-day, relentlessly following one fad after another. That constant changing of style is part of the need to find themselves, to work out who they are, and for some it betrays a lack of confidence.

You *can* fight age, just as you can fight your shape, your face, your bones and your hair, but you must be careful how you do it: you don't want to embody the stereotype of mutton dressed as lamb. You could accept that ageing is inevitable and give up altogether. Or you could stop thinking in terms of years, and concentrate on *yourself*: a person who, like everyone else, is changing.

How do you think you should look? You might enjoy going back to the questions on page 17, answering them again as if you were 20 or 30, and seeing how they compare with you now.

Curiously enough it's not your clothes that make you look older. Out-of-date hair and 10-year-old make-up, however becoming they once were, are very ageing indeed. Just think about turquoise eyeshadow, heavy black eyelashes and pinky-white lipstick, topped with a beehive hairdo!

What the 70s have offered the older woman is the freedom to choose what suits her from a wide range of styles. And today's

▲ *Leslie Caron, a film star beauty in her youth, demonstrates the art of understatement. The simple hairstyle and casual clothes only accentuate her striking features.*

make-up is perfect for greying hair and ageing skin—a healthy natural face with a bit of what used to be called rouge, a touch of eyeliner and mascara with gentle shadowing (bright eyes gain emphasis as hair goes white), and a warm, rosy lip colour. And remember what the great cosmetic queen Helena Rubenstein said about skin: only neglect is ageing.

Avoid anything that makes you look droopy. Hair with a side parting and soft waves looks far younger than a long, straight style; what you are after are soft lines and uplift. As your hair gets greyer, even white, you will find gentle colours in your make-up more flattering than, for example, dramatic red lipstick.

Similarly, the colours you used to favour for clothes may not now suit you so well, in particular dull tones like navy, maroon and